The Way We Were

Runcorn Remembered: A Social History

by
Liz Howard

First published 1993
Reprinted 1997

Distributed by   The Curiosity Bookshop
                  52 High Street
                  Runcorn
                  WA7 1AW

Cover photograph: *The Transporter Bridge across the Manchester Ship Canal.*

ISBN 1 85926 031 4

Printed and bound by   MFP Design & Print
                        Longford Trading Estate
                        Thomas Street
                        Stretford
                        Manchester
                        M32 0JT
                        Tel: 0161–864 4540

This book is dedicated to Jack.
A Runcorn lad.

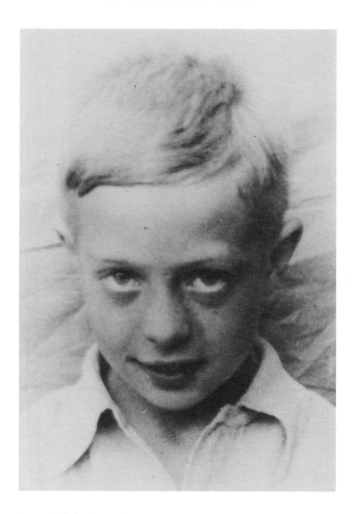

Born 20th October 1924. Educated at All Saints Parish School. Died by drowning in the River Mersey in February 1942, aged seventeen years four months. The vessel on which he worked sank, fully laden, during a storm in the hours of darkness.

In 1850, Thomas Lyon, Gilbert Greenall and Edward Greenall drew up an agreement allowing Samuel Collier, a Runcorn grocer, to build property on their land in High Street. It wasn't until 1st May, 1870 that the premises of 52 High Street and the adjoining cottages in Back High Street were built and sold to John Hedgecock. He plied his trade as a barber at his shop in High Street until his death in April, 1884, when he left it in his will to his wife and children — "Except my son Charles, who in my opinion has already had his share."

Through the years the shop has had many owners and a variety of uses, but is probably best remembered as the Gem Stores, owned for almost forty years by Mr and Mrs James Smith Terretta.

In 1988, aged 82 years, Mr Terretta decided to retire, and his fascinating shop where anything from Union Jacks to tea-pot lids could be found, was bought by Liz and Brian Howard. After complete renovation and refitting, the shop, now incorporating the adjoining row of cottages, was opened as the Curiosity Bookshop on 1st May, 1990. This book is written at the request, and with the help of, its customers.

INTRODUCTION

Once upon a time, Runcorn was a small village centred round a clear stream wending its way towards the River Mersey; a gateway into Lancashire via the ferryman for Cheshire folk, farmers and their produce. When the Duke of Bridgewater built his canal there were grumbles from the farmers about the difficulty of carts trying to negotiate steep bridges over the offending canal on their way to the ferry. Runcorn was being cut off.

When the Manchester Ship Canal was built, there were grumbles about the impossibility of trading across the river. Runcorn was being cut off.

When the new road bridge was built, expressways and busways criss-crossed the ancient town in every direction turning it into a patchwork of bits and pieces without a proper heart, while three miles away the Shopping City grew from green fields to cater for the New Town. Runcorn was most definitely cut off. Many of the migrants were unaware of Runcorn's old heart and it seemed fated to wither and die. But Runcorn is a family town older than Liverpool, populated with the descendents of the original villagers who had watched the first of those changes and the building of the Bridgewater Canal. For generations they held their ground in the face of successive invasions, marrying the newcomers and integrating them into the community, turning them into Runcornians. Even today the shops are mainly family owned, many traders following fathers and grandfathers, dispensing service with a smile to customers who have become friends. A town is only as strong as its people. So Runcorn lives, despite everything, and if we examine those who built it and stayed to see it prosper, perhaps we can understand why.

LIST OF CONTRIBUTORS

Mr Bate	Mrs Bellard
Mr Bennett	Mr Betley
Mr Braverman	Mr Tom Brown
Mrs Clarke	Mr Caulfield
Mrs Clear	Mr Done
Mr Edwards	Mr Fitton
Mr Ford	Mr Garner
Mr J Gough	Mr R Gough
Mr Greatorex	Mr Hamilton
Mr Hayes	Mr Hignett
Mr K Holt	Mr T Holt
Mr Littlemore	Mr Littler
Mr Lloyd	Mr Macleod
Mrs Marsh	May Martin
Mrs Millinger	Mr Morton
Mr Nurse	Mrs Oakes
Mr Peacock	Mrs Pendlebury
Mrs Platt	Mrs Prince
Mrs Purslow	Mr Shallcross
Mr Sweetman	Mrs Thompson
Mrs Wakefield	Mr Walker
Mrs Watson	Mrs Whitney
Mr Wilks	

My thanks to them for their help.

When Mary Whitlow presented her husband Samuel Watson with a daughter, Hannah, in 1842, Runcorn had a population of less than five thousand. Salmon and shrimp could be caught in the clear waters of the Mersey, and the ancient Parish Church watched benevolently as the folk of the town crossed and recrossed the Runcorn Gap in the capable hands of the ferryman, as they had for four hundred years, even in the depths of winter.

HANNAH WATSON.

FERRY HUT FEATURED ON AN EARLY CHRISTMAS CARD.

Times were changing. Only five years after Hannah's baptism the foundation stone for a new church was laid on the site of the old. Within two years, an elegant spire soared heavenwards and a new landmark had been created.

Some of the stone used in the construction had been hewn from Runcorn's quarries where men with muscle could always find a day's work.

RUNCORN PARISH CHURCH

RUNCORN HILL

OLD HALL,
HIGH STREET

Local sandstone could be seen in many of the larger dwellings in the area and news of its qualities and the town of its origin spread far and wide. The foundation stone for the Anglican Cathedral in Liverpool was taken from the Runcorn quarries.

BROOKFIELD FARM,
HIGHER RUNCORN

Owen Jones, working in the quarries of Snowdonia, heard of the money to be made in the growing industries of Runcorn. Moving his wife and six children from their native Anglesey, the family arrived with few belongings to find a town spilling over from its centre around Delph Bridge.

MARY ROBERTS.

STONE STREET, OFF BRIDGE STREET. MRS CAULFIELD STANDS ON THE STEP OF HER COTTAGE. SHE ALSO OWNED THE OTHERS IN THE ROW, RENTING THEM OUT TO THE BOAT PEOPLE OF THE BRIDGEWATER CANAL FOR FIVE SHILLINGS PER WEEK.

HALTON GRANGE, BUILT IN 1854 BY SOAP WORKS OWNER THOMAS JOHNSON AS HIS PRIVATE RESIDENCE. IT BECAME RUNCORN TOWN HALL IN 1932

It was a town full of the smell of tanneries and soap-works and breweries. There were boat-yards and sailmakers, slate works and timber-yards, brick-works, foundries and a works for the manufacture of caustic soda.

In 1861 Mary Whitlow died and was buried in one of the first graves to be dug in the new cemetery in Greenway Road. Shortly afterwards, her daughter Hannah married Thomas Marsh. That same year plans were put into operation for the construction of the railway bridge to provide a line between London and the great port of Liverpool. The building of the bridge began two years later and Thomas Marsh obtained work as a labourer on the project. He didn't live to see the first train cross the Mersey, but fell to his death leaving behind a young widow and two babies.

Two years later Hannah married John Percival by whom she had six children.

THE RUNCORN RAILWAY BRIDGE AND PARISH CHURCH SEEN FROM WIDNES.

Recognised first as part of the port of Liverpool and later the Port of Manchester, shipping formed an important part of the town's life and boat-building produced a skilled work-force.

HMS DESPATCH — THE LAST SHIP TO BE LAUNCHED FROM BRUNDITT & HAYES BOATYARD, MERSEY ROAD, BEFORE THE BUILDING OF THE MANCHESTER SHIP CANAL.

FERRY HUT, STILL PROMINENT DURING THE CONSTRUCTION OF THE MANCHESTER SHIP CANAL.

In 1887, when the first sod was cut for the construction of the Manchester Ship Canal, the future of the town as a commercial centre was assured.

Along with thousands of others, Mary Robert's son-in-law, John Cooke, found work with the construction gangs and in 1894 the waterway was opened to traffic.

THE FAIRY QUEEN CROWDED WITH SIGHTSEERS ON THE CANAL AT LATCHFORD.

Housing for the growing population had spread to the land beyond the Railway Bridge to Duke's Fields. Those moving into the rented properties included Elizabeth Jones and her husband John Cooke. The main leisure activity for the men after working long, hard hours was a night in the Pub. On occasion, when Jack found himself locked in the cells at Runcorn Police Station on a Saturday night after a brawl, his wife would take him a hot Sunday lunch between two plates as he waited for the Monday Magistrate.

These two-up, two-down cottages held large families. Gas lighting took over from oil lamps and candles early in the century, to be followed by electricity in the 1930's and 1940's. Mrs Caulfield, renting out her cottages in Stone Street was then able to increase the rent to six shillings per week. Washing was done in a dolly-tub in the back yard and the toilet was a bucket situated in a closet in the yard. These were emptied regularly by the night-soil men traversing the back entries with their carts. A generation later, water was laid on to each house and main drains were put in. Toilets were simply vertical pipes let into these drains, flushed only when waste water from the slop-stone or sink ran away down the same drain.

JOHN COOKE AND HIS FOUR CHILDREN OUTSIDE THIER DUKES FIELD HOME.

DUKES FIELDS AND THE CANAL.

A footbridge constructed as part of the railway bridge was fine for pedestrians and cyclists, but the construction of the Manchester Ship Canal finally put an end to the ancient ferry boat. There was no way across the River Mersey for road traffic at Runcorn until the problem was solved by the magnificent Transporter Bridge. It was opened in 1905 by Sir John Brunner of the Brunner-Mond Chemical Company, later to become ICI.

SIR JOHN BRUNNER CROSSING THE MERSEY BY CAR VIA THE TRANSPORTER

THE TRANSPORTER BRIDGE

TRANSPORTER CAR 1905

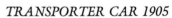

Manchester Spinner is guided
along the Manchester Ship
Canal at Runcorn, passing
under the Transporter Bridge.

17

The Transporter Bridge was popular with both passengers and those who like to watch the world go by. Ferry Hut and the area behind it, once known as Angel Fields, was a popular playground for the young until recent times, the river traffic providing an interesting and ever-changing spectacle.

HOLIDAY TIME AT FERRY HUT.

TUGS AT OLD QUAY YARD.

SAND DREDGER.

TUG, VICEROY.

PADDLE TUG.

*LARGE VESSEL WITH
HALTON CASTLE IN
THE BACKGROUND.*

SPRINCH BOATYARD.

BIG POOL IN HEATH ROAD.

This was the site of the Sprinch Boatyard, workplace for generations of the same families, including Mr Holt and his son.

One of the ancient landmarks not far from the centre of Runcorn was Big Pool near the junction of Heath Road and Victoria Road.

WORKERS AT SPRINCH BOATYARD c.1910.

After the main building was destroyed by fire, work repairing barges ceased and many will remember Big Pool as the graveyard it became.

For thirty years the wooden door and the stone steps of the main entrance remained as a sad memorial to the past. Now these too are gone.

BIG POOL WITH BURNT-OUT BUILDING IN BACKGROUND

THE DOOR TO NOWHERE

Grieg's sail loft in Waterloo Road no longer houses the large workforce needed for a town built on rivercraft. Family tradition survives, however, and today's Mr Grieg still works as a sailmaker in Runcorn, thanks to local yachtsmen. The smaller premises are situated appropriately enough at the Mariner's Mission Hall.

GREIG'S SAIL-LOFT, WATERLOO ROAD.

GREIG'S SAIL-LOFT.

AT WORK IN GREIG'S SAIL-LOFT.

With its dairy herds and forests, the tanning of leather was a well-established industry in rural Cheshire when the Bridgewater Canal was built, and as there was then no substitute for real leather, tanneries soon became big business. Runcorn's canals were used for delivering the raw materials of coal, raw hides and tree bark, and for the removal of the fine tanned hides. Much of the leather was used for kitting out Britain's vast Victorian army with boots, belts and horse tackle. At the turn of the century, Runcorn was Britain's largest leather producer, processing more than ten thousand hides per week.

The workforce was local and, as on the canals, served by generations of the same families, marrying and inter-marrying. By this time the Jones's children had grown and married and had families of their own. Hannah's eldest son, too, had married and produced a daughter. It was the kind of town where everyone knew everyone and marriages ensured that most families were at least distant relatives of each other. Tannery workers were no exception and workmates became friends as companies provided social entertainment outside working hours.

*CAMDEN CHAPEL
CONCERT PARTY*

*HIGHFIELD TANNERY
WORKFORCE*

*TANNERY CROWNS THE
CORONATION CEREMONY, 1953*

Some of the hides used by the tanneries must have come from the Percival Lane slaughter house, where it was not unusual for a man to take his animal to be killed before selling it as meat in his shop. Even in the nineteen-forties, pigs were driven squealing through the streets from No-Man's-Land at the edge of the canal into Percival Lane. The name may be a coincidence, but one of the greatest delicacies of those days were Percival's sausages, made from a closely guarded recipe and sold in a shop in Church Street. The decline of the tanneries began in the 1960's with the introduction of man-made subsitutes and one of Runcorn's great industries was lost.

MR WORRALL WITH HIS ANIMAL.

MR WORRAL IN HIS BUTCHERS SHOP, BRIDGE STREET.

BAILEY'S BUTCHER'S, CHURCH STREET.

RILEY'S GROCERY SHOP IN BRIDGE STREET, LATER TO BECOME A BAKERY WHICH WAS ONLY DEMOLISHED WITH THE ADVENT OF THE NEW TOWN.

HALTON VILLAGE ACROSS THE FIELDS.

Before the First World War, countryside was only a short walk from the town. The old quarries were becoming overgrown with grass and heather, the raw red of the sandstone becoming dark with the smoke of the ever-expanding chemical industry.

MOUGHLAND LANE.

At Weston Point, farm land ran right down to the Canal, animals grazing peacefully on the lush grasses.

Crops were still being harvested at Weston Point after the beginnings of a Chemical Company began building beside the Manchester Ship Canal. The company later became ICI.

FARM CROPS AT WESTON POINT.

WESTON POINT.

Cottage Hospital, Runcorn.

The Cottage Hospital is now used as offices and a larger modern hospital has been built in the Halton Village area on what used to be open countryside.

In 1943, this little girl, great-great grandaughter of Hannah and Mary, was still able to pick daisies in the fields of Picow Farm Road, the houses of Adela Road in the background. The area is now a Bridge approach road and industrial estate.

31

POWER HOUSE, ICI

By the nineteen fifties the ICI factory stretched for over two miles along the canal side, having built its own huge Power House to generate electricity.

With tanneries and boat-yards in decline, ICI took over the role of major employer in the area with a work-force of over 5000 men and women. These were mainly local people and despite its size, the company maintained a family atmosphere until the nineteen seventies. Gifts were presented not only for long service, but on the occasion of marriage.

WEDDING GIFTS

PRESENTATION DURING TEA-BREAK.

ICI PARTY

ICI PARTY

Such was the family atmosphere within ICI that workers' children looked forward to a magnificent Christmas party every year where they had plenty to eat, games to play and a gift from Father Christmas himself at the end of the day.

THE PARK LAKE AT THE TURN OF THE CENTURY.

RUNCORN WATERWORKS ACROSS THE PARK LAKE.

The Waterworks Superintendent pictured in front of his place of work was George Littlemore, a man born in Kingsley in 1852. He married Mary Ann Hughes at St Paul's Church, Runcorn, and lived with her and their six children in one of the Park Cottages. It was a brisk two minute walk from his front door to his office.

In the early years of the century, Runcorn was a great Liberal stronghold on the political front, and the election of Sir John Brunner as Member of Parliament was a great occasion. The result was read from the balcony of the Liberal Club in Regent Street to crowds packed in like sardines.

THE CAPTION READS: MAJORITY 1792.
THE GLAD TIDINGS BEING READ.

ST. PAUL'S CHURCH, HIGH STREET, NOW THE SITE OF A HEALTH CENTRE.

This postcard was sent to Mrs Parry in Bristol from someone called Mary, possibly her sister, in Runcorn. It reads: Duncan in the window and Frank on the left waving something in his hand. Next Wed. Mr Unsworth is being ordained at St. Paul's and a month after he sails for India to be a missionary.

But in 1914, the young men of the town left on a mission far less peaceful. Many, with their knowlege of ropes, sails and ships, joined the navy, including Mary Robert's grandson, Jack Cooke, junior.

SARAH MARSH

Jack was actively involved in the Battle of Jutland but returned safely to marry his sweetheart, Sarah Marsh. Thus, the families of Hannah and Mary, typical of their day, were united.

NAVAL VOLUNTEERS. JACK COOKE, AGE SIXTEEN, STANDING FAR LEFT. HE LIED ABOUT HIS AGE IN ORDER TO BECOME AN ABLE SEAMAN.

Other young men joined the army, incuding Albert Bowman, a print worker in the Print Works in High Street.

Many years later, during the Second World War, the print works in High Street was used as a training centre but as the top floor was thought to be unsafe, it was used for recreation. Those wanting to enjoy themselves in war-time did so at their own risk!

Albert was killed in action in 1917, only six weeks after landing in France, his name being inscribed on the newly erected War Memorial at the top of Greenway Road. His daughter Ethel later ran a chip shop in the town.

ALBERT BOWMAN WITH HIS WIFE AND DAUGHTER.

SNOOKER TABLES IN THE OLD PRINT WORKS.

THE CENOTAPH.

Thomas Alfred Jones of Princess Street, Runcorn was better known as Todjer Jones. On 20th September 1917, whilst fighting the enemy, he caught sight of a sniper firing at the British troops. Moving through heavy barrage, a bullet went through his helmet and another through his coat. He shot the sniper dead, whereupon two other Germans rose into view waving a white flag. Having been warned of this trick, Todjer shot and killed both of them. The rest of the Germans in the trench surrendered to Todjer and when he finally marched them back as prisoners, it was found that he had captured 102 enemy soldiers, including three or four officers single handed. Todjer was not one to rest on his laurels and later carried a total of five messages between Companies under heavy fire. He was awarded the Victoria Cross and the Distinguished conduct Medal for his bravery.

On the open space of the Park another, more explicit memorial was raised. All the young people of the day knew The Tank well, and it became a recognised meeting place. Many a stolen kiss was exchanged in its shadow and for the younger ones it was a place of make-believe, to climb on and hide in.

TODJER JONES.

THE TANK.

BILLY MORTON (ON DRUMS) AND HIS BAND.

Dances were regularly held in the town, even in war-time. There were several popular venues including the Guild Hall in Greenway Road and the Devonshire Cafe, Devonshire Square, affectionately known as the Dev. Billy Morton was well known both in the town and further afield, Joe Loss, the famous band-leader being a personal friend.

The Scala Cinema, never up to the standard of the other local cinema, was converted to a dance hall and, with the end of the Brunswick, Runcorn people, young and old, flocked to dance to the music of Stan Clarke and his Band, many a romance blossoming under the glittering globe suspended from the centre of the ceiling.

THE SCALA.

The Scala Ballroom is no more, the building having been converted into a Bingo Hall.

STAN CLARKE AND HIS BAND.

RUNCORN ROCK N' ROLLERS.

THE BRUNSWICK HALL SET OUT FOR THE WEDDING FEAST OF LILIAN SHALLCROSS AND FRED MATTRAVERS c.1923.

Weddings were celebrated as part of the natural order of things in those days, living in sin and single parenthood bringing disgrace to respectable families. The Brunswick Hall had been built in Brunswick Street, off Mersey Road, as a Victorian schoolroom, but later it was used as a Sunday School, community hall and war-time soup kitchen. In the late 1950's a new musical sound arrived in Britain from America and Runcorn's teenagers rocked and rolled to the music of Don Moremon and his Band, featuring Dave Morton, son of Billy, on the drums. At the interval, orange squash was served as dancing continued to all the latest records. This was the grand finale for the old hall and it was demolished in the early sixties. Although Teddy Boys had a reputation for violence, there was little evidence of any real criminal activity in Runcorn. Young people dressed up in the fashion of the times for bravado and mostly clean fun.

DANCERS AT THE SATURDAY NIGHT HOP.

A GROUP OF MRS WILKINSON'S ROCK N' ROLLERS ON A DAY TRIP TO TRENTHAM GARDENS IN 1957. MRS WILKINSON SECOND FROM RIGHT, FRONT ROW.

STALL-HOLDERS INSIDE THE MARKET HALL
c.1905.

Like the Brunswick and the Scala, the Market Hall, built in 1856 in Bridge Street, has also fulfilled a variety of roles.

THE MARKET HALL.

MANNEQUIN PARADE c.1926 INSIDE THE MARKET HALL.

By the time this mannequin parade was in progress, the Market Hall had already been converted to make a Public Swimming Baths during the summer months, the pool being covered by wooden flooring during the winter enabling the hall to be used for other purposes. The market stalls were relegated to a covered area outside the swimming baths in Bridge Street.

*THE PUBLIC
SWIMMING BATHS.*

*THE OUTSIDE MARKET,
BRIDGE STREET.*

Some of the ladies and gentleman watching the fashion show also enjoyed travelling further afield.

Two decades later, with the euphoria of Germany's defeat fading, disillusionment set in and Runcornians of all political persuasions joined the great exodus to the New World. Councillor George Lowe and his wife Olwen were amongst those taking up the offer of transport to Australia for just £10 each.

LADIES OF THE CONSERVATIVE CLUB ON THEIR ANNUAL OUTING. FURTHER COPIES OF THE PHOTOGRAPH COULD BE OBTAINED FOR 1/-.

THE LOCAL LABOUR PARTY SAYS GOODBYE TO COUNCILLOR LOWE.

CHILDREN LINE THE ROYAL ROUTE C.1927.

Despite King Edward VII having to cancel his appointment to open the Transporter Bridge, Runcorn was occasionally visited by Royalty.

KING GEORGE V IS GREETED BY MAYOR GITTINS.

When the motor car first appeared on Runcorn's streets, Mr Walker of Walker's Garage was enterprising enough to build his own. He is seen here about to take his sister for a spin.

MR WALKER AND HIS SISTER IN HIS CAR

WALKER'S GARAGE AT THE BOTTOM OF GREENWAY ROAD BY THE CLEVELAND CORNER

THE CLEVELAND PUB, GREENWAY ROAD.

Kings and garage owners excepted, owning a car was something of an impossible dream. For most, motorised transport meant catching a bus from the Cleveland.

On the bottom side of the Cleveland was Lowlands Road, now only a memory, and that well-known landmark the Bijou, pronounced Beejoo in French but always known as the By-joe in Runcorn. The smell of rich dark tobacco seeped out through the open door to tempt all passers-by.

THE BIJOU

A few yards further along was Woods's Garage, and next to that was the best cinema in town, The Empress. Two films per night, two programmes per week.

WOOD'S GARAGE.

THE EMPRESS CINEMA.

PIGHUE LANE,
LOOKING
TOWARDS THE
RAILWAY
HOTEL IN
LOWLANDS
ROAD.

The ruined building next to the cinema had faded writing on the wall proclaiming it to be the Vine Hotel, though few, if any could remember it ever being such an establishment.

The yard behind the Vine Hotel and the buildings in Pighue Lane, off Lowlands Road, were originally used as stables, being adjacent to the Bridgewater Canal with its horse-drawn barges.

THE VINE HOTEL
AT THE TURN OF THE CENTURY.

Horse-drawn barges on the Bridgewater Canal eventually gave way to powered craft carrying a variety of cargoes and these were plentiful even in the 1940's.

APPROACHING DELPH BRIDGE.

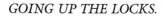

GOING UP THE LOCKS.

TOP LOCKS.

LOCKS APPROACHING WATERLOO BRIDGE.

THE TOP LOCK.

One of the more sinister sides of living in a town surrounded by water was the danger from drowning, a far more frequent occurence in the days of heavy water traffic. Men, women and children have all disappeared into the murky depths, leaving the Grappling Corps the gruesome task of recovering the bodies, though they also grappled for lost cargo.

A well-known figure on the canal until the early 1970s was a character called Charlie Atkins, often titled Chocolate Charlie. He was one of the last of the old boat people in the area and this is a rare photograph of him.

CHARLIE ATKINS.

*MERSEY MISSION
GRAPPLING CORPS
WITH MINISTER
MR SHAW.*

CROFTON LODGE.

The pharmaceutical industry, like Charlie, has left the area. Evans Biological Institute was situated in Penn Lane where Crofton Lodge, built in 1783, was adapted in 1902 for use as a laboratory. It was here that the revolutionary smallpox vaccine was first made on a commercial basis, the work carried out in Runcorn saving millions of lives world-wide and wiping out the killer disease for ever. The memory of the original house lingers only in the name of near-by Crofton Road.

The company built the largest stable in Britain at Runcorn to house the horses needed to produce serum for anti-toxins, the fore-runners of antibiotics, as part of the war effort. There were up to 485 horses kept there at any one time.

WOMEN AT WORK PACKAGING THE PRODUCTS.

HORSES BEING BLED. THE MAN IN THE FORE-GROUND IS OWEN DAVIES OF RUNCORN.

The packing department was destroyed by fire in 1945 when a build-up of gases was accidently ignited. One man was killed and several badly burned.

THE AIR RAID PATROL.

In 1939, many of Runcorn's young men were again called to serve their country but this time, for those left at home there was an added fear of bombs from the air. Men not allowed to join the Army, Navy or Airforce became Runcorn's defence at home, some joining the Home Guard and others, the Air Raid Patrol.

In those terrifying times strange craft were frequently seen gliding along the Manchester Ship Canal.

SUBMARINE ON THE
MANCHESTER SHIP CANAL.

THE HOME GUARD.

57

Women took on men's jobs to keep the wheels rolling , including these three who trained as clippies to work on Runcorn's buses.

The end of the war was celebrated with street parties, long tables being laid out in the street, and though in that era of ration-books there was no ice-cream, there were plenty of fairy cakes, nearly-set jellies, and cups of tea from giant tea pots.

CLAIRE THOMPSON, LEFT,
HELEN GALLIGAN, CENTRE,
PEARL O'CALLAHAN, RIGHT.

HANDLEY STREET PARTY.

THE MAYOR
OPENS THE
PARTY.

After the Second World War the people of Runcorn were determined to build a better life for their children. They worked hard in a spirit of community and hope, and eventually life began to improve. Food in the shops became more varied, though ration books would be needed for some years, as the notice in Irwin's window shows.

STAFF AT IRWIN'S GROCERS, CHURCH STREET, C.1946.

Only five years later the shelves were almost full, with chocolate and eggs on top of the counter instead of hidden under it.

MELIA'S GROCERY, C.1951.

*FLETCHER'S, MAYPOLE
AND HARGREAVE'S IN
HIGH STREET. C.1955.*

*HIGH STREET, LOOKING
TOWARDS BRIDGE STREET.*

*CANAL STREET COTTAGES BY
THE STEPS TO DELPH BRIDGE.*

All these buildings have now been
demolished to make way for the new,
as have many houses, pubs and
churches in this area of town.

The shoemakers of Runcorn hit hard
times when leather substitutes arrived
on the market and large firms like ICI
gave contracts for industrial footwear to
outside companies. Mr Moss, finding it
hard to make ends meet, chopped
firewood, selling it in bundles from a cart
he pulled round the streets with the help
of his small daughter. In those days there
were few social benefits and men did
what they could, however they could, to
earn an honest living.

*POVEY'S SHOE REPAIRERS, ONCE
OWNED BY THE FAMOUS 'CLOGGER'
MOSS'S FAMILY, AT THE CORNER OF
PENKETH'S LANE, OFF HIGH STREET.*

*THE OLD QUARRY WALL,
DELPH BRIDGE, ORIGINAL
SITE OF RUNCORN TOWN.*

HALTON ROAD
METHODIST CHAPEL.

INSIDE HALTON ROAD
METHODIST CHAPEL.

BETHESDA CHURCH, HIGH STREET.

CAMDEN METHODIST CHURCH.

LORD RODNEY,
CHURCH STREET.

THE MASONIC, OFTEN
CALLED THE LONG
PULL, IS STILL IN
DEVONSHIRE SQUARE,
BUT STUNTED NOW
WITHOUT THE TOP FLOOR.

THE LONDON AND NORTH
WESTERN PUB, LOWLANDS
ROAD.

THE OLD RAILWAY STATION
PICTURED AT THE TURN OF THE
CENTURY AND 50 YEARS LATER, IS
NOW ALSO A THING OF THE PAST.

PUPILS AT VICTORIA ROAD SCHOOL.

These pupils in the early part of the century at Victoria Road School would still recognise their place of learning today, from the outside, at least. The School fought and won the battle for refurbishment rather than demolition.

Other pupils would not be so lucky.

PUPILS AT THE PARISH SCHOOL, 1928. BETTY COOKE, A DESCENDANT OF MARY AND HANNAH, SITS CROSS-LEGGED, FRONT ROW RIGHT.

ALL SAINTS PARISH SCHOOL,
CHURCH STREET.

SIDE VIEW OF
ALL SAINTS
PARISH
SCHOOL
DURING
DEMOLITION.

ALL SAINT'S PARISH CHURCH CHOIR PROCESSING TO THE CHURCH FOR THE INDUCTION OF THE NEW VICAR, REV BRASNETT c.1944. THE COTTAGES ON THE LEFT WERE DEMOLISHED TO MAKE WAY FOR THE NEW PRIMARY SCHOOL.

CANON BRASNETT WITH MEMBERS OF THE MOTHER'S UNION, MEETING IN CHURCH HOUSE, CHURCH STREET

THE CONFIRMATION CLASS OF 1979, IN ST JOHN'S CHURCH, WESTON, WITH REV KEN PRITCHARD, MAYOR ARTHUR PARR AND MRS PARR.

One aspect of community life has centred around the churches of the town, and in looking at the contrast between old and new it can be seen that many non-conformist establishments have disappeared, including: St Paul's Wesleyan Methodist, Halton Road Wesleyan Methodist, Brunswick Chapel, Camden Methodist, Primitive Methodist Chapel, and Bethesda Chapel, High Street. Many of the surviving churches such as All Saints, Holy Trinity, St Michaels and All Angels and St John's, Weston owe allegiance to the Church of England, with the smaller Roman Catholic population moving from Windmill Street to the new church in Ivy Street in 1956. The building of the New Town outside the old town boundaries has necessitated new churches of both denominations in these areas.

THE BRAVERMAN FAMILY.

The Jewish community in Runcorn was small, consisting for many years of a single family. Benjemin Braverman deserted from the Russian Army and the problems of being a Russian Jew at the turn of the century, to escape with his wife Liza firstly to Paris, and then to England. They settled in Runcorn and set themselves up in business without being able to speak a word of English. Benjamin was a fine cabinet maker and his elder son Myer later converted the shop in High Street into an antiques business. Rose was an expert on antiquarian books. The business continued until Harry, the surviving member of the family, retired in 1991.

PARISH SCHOOL FOOTBALL
TEAM, 1927, WITH MR
DAVIES AND HEADMASTER
MR LINDSAY. THE TEAM
INCLUDES SIMCOCK,
CLUCAS, MCDONALD,
CLAYS, TONKS, COX,
RATCLIFFE, PRESCOTT,
EVANS, BAZLEY AND
SHALLCROSS.

VICTORIA ROAD SCHOOL WAS
ALSO THE SCENE OF TOM
BROWN'S SCHOOLDAYS, THAT
BEING THE NAME OF THE BOY
SECOND LEFT, BACK ROW
BEHIND MR ROBINSON, THE
HEADMASTER. C.1943).

Granville Street School was demolished to make way for a new outside market in the centre of the shopping area between Church Street and High Street. This picture, taken at Granville Street School in September, 1948 may be typical of school classes everywhere. Many grew up, married locally and remained in or near the town to raise their families, but at least two went to Australia and one to Canada, spreading the Runcorn spirit worldwide, as had the previous generation. One of the Australian émigrés won the National Lottery and made himself a fortune. Many of those who stayed worked for ICI in offices and laboratories and on production plants. The class also produced an accountant, a school teacher, a school secretary, a market gardener, a Jehovah's Witness, a refuse disposal officer and an author. One had eight children, and one was murdered.

In 1948 these children still lived in the two-up, two-down cottages of the town, but by now they had the benefit of electric light and flush-toilets in the yard. Bath night was still the tin bath in front of the fire, filled from pans of water heated on a gas ring. In the streets outside their homes they played games such as marbles, jacks and hop-scotch and a day out was a walk to Runcorn Hill, the former quarries, with a bag of jam butties.

Many in the town have fond memories of yet another demolished building, Balfour Road Secondary School.

And the old school-room at Weston has gone the same way, the descendants of this Weston football team of 1926–27, seen outside the old sand-stone building, now enjoying the comforts of a modern building.

BALFOUR ROAD SCHOOL.

WESTON FOOTBALL TEAM, 1926–27.

The youth of Runcorn have long been known as football players.

At the turn of the century, however, the town was known more for its Rugby, Dick Padbury, the captain in this picture of the club, being capped for England. Descendents of his sister's family still live in Weston Village.

RUNCORN AFC, 1906–07

RUNCORN RFC

RUNCORN AFC 1961-62 SHOWING THE WINNERS OF THE CHESHIRE SENIOR CUP: ANDERS, C CUNNINGHAM, FERRIDAY, PENDLEBURY, R WILLIAMS, DEREK JONES, BOOTHWAY (MANAGER), KELLY, D JONES, LAWMAN, FOSTER, S CUNNINGHAM (CAPT), MOSS, J WILLIAMS.

RUNCORN BOWLING LEAGUE 1912.

Steeplechase and the British Games Steeplechase, being presented with his trophy by HRH The Duke of Edinburgh. Trevor Holt owned a sports and tobacconist shop in Regent Street, Runcorn, and is a descendant of the boat-builders of the Sprinch boat-yard.

Another popular sport has always been bowls and there were several bowling greens in the town. In 1927 Percy Ainscough, a shoe-repairer by trade, won the British Crown Green Bowls Championship.

A year before Percy's triumph, Joe Earlam had won the English Amateur Billiards Championship, and in 1939 Trevor Holt won a unique double with the Warrington Junior and Senior Cross-country Championships. The war interrupted Trevor's sporting career but in 1949 he won the AAA

RUNCORN BOWLING CLUB c.1930, *FORMER MAYOR GITTENS PRESENTING PRIZES.*

TREVOR HOLT AT WHITE CITY 1949.

For earlier generations holidays took the form of a day trip, often to Rhyl or New Brighton, as was the case with these scouts on their way to the Soap Box Derby in 1956.

For others in the same organisation there was the excitement of a week under canvas.

RUNCORN SCOUTS SET OUT FOR NEW BRIGHTON.

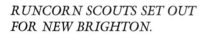

SCOUT CAMP AT HALTON c.1932.

VISITORS TO HALTON SCOUT CAMP.

SETTING OFF FOR CAMP C.1958.

And of course, there was always a good turn-out for the St George's Day Parade.

CUB SCOUTS AND LEADERS IN THE PARADE

In Runcorn, parades had for many generations been something of a way of life, bringing together people from all over the town to take part and to spectate at events ranging from funerals to carnivals.

Every policeman in the town turned out for the funeral of the Sergeant, found shot dead in the police station. His son was at first accused of the murder but no one was ever convicted.

POLICEMAN'S FUNERAL PROCESSION IN GREENWAY ROAD AT THE TURN OF THE CENTURY.

Most of the violence in the town until recent times was domestic, largely brought on by drink. Many a man would arrive home from the pub fighting drunk and if he didn't fight the next-door neighbour, it was his own wife and children. The non-conformist churches, particularly the Methodists, preached long and loud against the Demon Drink in the hope of putting an end to the violence, without which the town would have been almost crime-free.

RUNCORN POLICE STATION, SCENE OF THE CRIME.

There were many funeral carriages in attendance at the funeral in 1911 of the W. Timmins, J.P., local foundry owner and major employer in the town. The grocer's shop Briscoe and Sadler seen in the background, later came to be owned by the Monks family who still trade in the town today. The name Briscoe brings to mind tasty savoury ducks, bought from the butcher's shop in Egerton Street. Bring your own basin if you want gravy!

FUNERAL OF LATE W. TIMMINS

Greenway Road is again crowded as the band of the Oddfellows turns into Norman Road on the occasion of their Jubilee. Edward Monks (brother and rival of the previously mentioned grocer) can be seen in the doorway of his shop on the corner of Byron Street.

ODDFELLOWS JUBILEE.

A picture taken in 1907 shows an even earlier parade on the occasion of the Co-op Annual Gala being led by the band past the police station towards High Street.

Chairman's Sunday was another reason to parade, these two pictures being from 1925 and 1926 respectively, the first on Savage's Bridge, the second in Greenway Road.

CO-OP ANNUAL GALA.

CHAIRMAN'S SUNDAY 1925.

CHAIRMAN'S SUNDAY 1926.

GREENWAY ROAD METHODISTS LED BY REV C S MORRIS.

For public support, however, there was nothing like the Whit Sunday Walks, the participants carrying bright banners before them, bands playing and the parade stretching through the town for miles as the whole population made its way to Higher Runcorn. In the area known as the Plantation, off Highlands Road children, were entertained with donkey rides. After World War Two, the Plantation was abandoned and later Whit Walks terminated on the Heath Park area, a large annual Funfair arriving to provide entertainment.

WHIT WALKERS IN
BRIDGE STREET, 1948.

ST EDWARDS WALK SHOWING
THE NOW DEMOLISHED
SCHOOL IN WINDMILL STREET.

WHIT WALKERS AT
UNSWORTH'S CORNER
c.1955. THE GENTLEMAN
LEADING RUNCORN
PARISH CHURCH SUNDAY
SCHOOL IS MR.
J. W. MITCHELL OF
WATERLOO ROAD.

ADULTS FROM ST PAUL'S CHURCH,
OUTSIDE GREENWAY COTTAGE.

PIONEER BAND,
BRIDGE STREET.

HOLY TRINITY AND RAGGED
SUNDAY SCHOOL BANNER
AT BRADLEY'S CORNER,
BRIDGE STREET.

The villages of Weston and Halton were always distinct populations, separated from the town by open fields. Both held their own village events, as well as joining in with those in Runcorn.

*WESTON ROSE
FETE, 1927*

*HALTON ROSE
FETE, 1952*

RUNCORN MAY QUEEN, 1906.

1937 MAY QUEEN CROWNED,

Much time and effort was put into the main Runcorn Carnival, the groups being formed from Sunday Schools, Scout and Guide Troops, Youth Groups, Dancing Schools, and Cadets, with individuals entering into the spirit of it all, dressing up to collect for charity.

In 1937, Nora Fish was crowned by Mrs Brooker, with Doris Wilkinson, the retiring Queen beside her on the stage.

Thirty five years later, their grandchildren dressed as the Rose Queen and her retinue arrive on a decorated lorry.

ROSE QUEEN AND RETINUE c.1972.

In the early days the Whit Monday donkeys also turned out for summer-time fun, seen here at the Co-op Carnival. For the Runcorn Carnival, each group usually took a different theme, rosettes being awarded by judges for the best dressed in various categories.

DONKEYS AT CO-OP CARNIVAL, 1926.

COWBOYS AND INDIANS OF THE RAGGED SCHOOL IN BRIDGE STREET.

ELLESMERE STREET SUNDAY SCHOOL WITH
FLORAL BICYCLES ON WATERLOO BRIDGE.

THE PEDLARS PARADE IN 1949.

CAMDEN SUNDAY SCHOOL BECOME
PIXIES AND FAIRIES FOR THE DAY.

MISS TANDY'S DANCING CLASS MET IN THE LIBERAL CLUB, REGENT STREET, SEEN HERE AS CINDERELLAS AND PRINCE CHARMINGS FOR THE CARNIVAL c.1951.

MILL BROW MISSION TURNED THEIR LORRY INTO A GYPSY CARAVAN IN 1974, SEEN HERE IN MERSEY ROAD.

Dressing up in a good cause was not always left to the children as Bill Grundy shows. Most of Runcorn would turn out to watch the Carnival pass through the town, throwing pennies onto the lorries and filling the collecting boxes thrust at them by those walking in the parade.

CHEERS!

When, as motor cars became more common, the Transporter Bridge could no longer cater for the volume of traffic trying to cross the River Mersey, a new bridge began to take shape alongside the old.

As road traffic increased, traffic on the Manchester Ship Canal declined. Transportation of goods along the Bridgewater Canal had ceased with the closing of the tanneries. The town was changing its size and shape again.

Many of the old streets where families had lived for generations were torn down to make way for the approach roads to the Bridge and a temporary roundabout was made where the Cleveland, the Bijou and Walker's Garage had once stood.

NEW ROAD BRIDGE RISING ABOVE THE TRANSPORTER.

TEMPORARY ROUNDABOUT IN GREENWAY ROAD TAKEN FROM GREENWAY ROAD CHAPEL.

SPRING STREET.

Plans were going ahead to make Runcorn into a New Town, bringing people from Liverpool to provide them with better housing. As part of this programme, whole streets were demolished and Runcorn prepared for a face-lift.

PENKETH'S LANE.

LOWLAND'S ROAD.

ALBERT STREET

94

The funeral parlour was demolished, but this is one industry that hasn't disappeared and a new site was found. Brian Findlow, the local stonemason continued his trade uninterrupted in Victoria Road, making headstones for the people of Runcorn just as his forebears did in 1861 for Mary Whitlow.

S. RIGBY, FUNERALS,
ALBERT STREET

THE STONEMASON
AT WORK

The family names in this book recur generation after generation and well-known faces appear in the crowds. Relatives abound, because most Runcornians are cousins several times removed, thanks to the canals and boatyards, the tanneries and chemical works that brought them together, and the community spirit that helped them to stay, even in the bad times. For those waiting for the last crossing of the Transporter, there was a feeling of relief as the new bridge stood ready. No more standing in all weathers for the next trip across the river. The Victorian construction had never made a profit and had cost a fortune in maintenance, and in those days the thought that Runcorn might become a tourist resort on the strength of that edifice, never crossed anyone's mind.

THE TRANSPORTER AND NEW BRIDGE TOGETHER.

The people gathering to see Princess Alexandra open the new bridge perhaps realised how much the town had changed in one hundred years. Industries and churches had come and gone. Tin baths had disappeared and holidays consisting of a bottle of water and a jam butty at Ferry Hut were only a memory. They had worked long and hard to improve the lives of their children and in doing so had changed Runcorn for ever. The fields were no more. Big Pool had vanished. Housing estates mushroomed on all sides. In ten short years the town doubled its population, just as it had one hundred years before. Thirty years after the opening of the new bridge and the huge increase in population, the children had grown and had children of their own. Despite better living conditions and increased social benefits crime in the town escalated. Where, in their grandparents' time there had been one murder every ten years, there would be two each year. Stabbings and assaults became regular occurances as theft became a way of life for some. House burglaries became common-place, shop-lifting was almost accepted as part of the penalty of trying to provide a service, and anything that could be stolen or vandalised, was. Drugs, alcohol and sheer greed all played their part, as did the new bridge and nearby motorways by making the town accessible and providing escape routes. Most thieves are under thirty. Most old people are afraid. This is what they worked so hard for.

WAITING FOR THE OPENING OF THE NEW BRIDGE.

In another hundred years life will have changed again. Some of the names in the town may be new but, many are rooted in the piece of land south of the River Mersey where the ferry-man plied his craft through stormy waters for 600 years. Runcorn and its people will survive. Somehow.

The pictures in this book have been donated by the people of Runcorn for the people of Runcorn, so that some can remember and others understand, the way we were.

THE RUNCORN-WIDNES BRIDGE ABOUT TO OPEN, BRINGING IN A NEW ERA, 1961.

Runcorn
in old picture postcards

BACK IN TIME

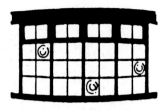